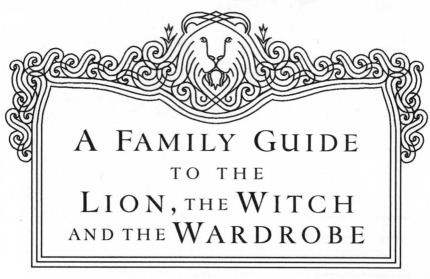

A FAMILY GUIDE
TO THE
LION, THE WITCH
AND THE WARDROBE

CHRISTIN DITCHFIELD

CROSSWAY BOOKS
A PUBLISHING MINISTRY OF
GOOD NEWS PUBLISHERS
WHEATON, ILLINOIS

A Family Guide to The Lion, the Witch and the Wardrobe

Published by Crossway Books
A publishing ministry of Good News Publishers
1300 Crescent Street
Wheaton, Illinois 60187

Illustrations: Justin Gerard, Portland Studios, Inc.
Design: The DesignWorks Group; cover & interior, Charles Brock; interior, Robin Black.
    www.thedesignworksgroup.com

First printing, 2005

Printed in the United States of America

LIBRARY OF CONGRESS CATALOGING-IN-PUBLICATION DATA

Ditchfield, Christin.
    A family guide to The lion, the witch and the wardrobe / Christin Ditchfield.
        p.   cm.
    ISBN 1-58134-725-1 (tpb)
        1. Lewis, C. S. (Clive Staples), 1898-1963. Lion, the witch, and the wardrobe.
    2. Children's stories, English—History and criticism. 3. Christian fiction, English—
    History and criticism. 4. Fantasy fiction, English—History and criticism. 5. Narnia
    (Imaginary place) I. Title.
    PR6023.E926L433 2005
    823'.912—dc22

                                                                            2005009873

DP 14   13   12   11   10   09   08   07   06   05

12 11   10   9   8   7   6   5   4   3   2   1

TABLE OF CONTENTS

Welcome to Narnia: An Introduction.............................5

Meet the Creator of Narnia: C. S. Lewis 11

Step into the Wardrobe 20

"The Story Within the Story" 27

CHAPTER ONE: Lucy Looks into a Wardrobe.................31

CHAPTER TWO: What Lucy Found There 35

CHAPTER THREE: Edmund and the Wardrobe...............37

CHAPTER FOUR: Turkish Delight...................................41

    Deadly Delights..43

CHAPTER FIVE: Back on This Side of the Door.............47

CHAPTER SIX: Into the Forest 49

CHAPTER SEVEN: A Day with the Beavers 53

CHAPTER EIGHT: What Happened After Dinner............56

    Is He Safe? 59

CHAPTER NINE: In the Witch's House 63

    The Path We Choose...65

CHAPTER TEN: The Spell Begins to Break 69

    Tools, Not Toys 71

CHAPTER ELEVEN: Aslan Is Nearer 75

CHAPTER TWELVE: Peter's First Battle............................77

    Winning Our Spurs...81

CHAPTER THIRTEEN: Deep Magic from the Dawn of Time..85

CHAPTER FOURTEEN: The Triumph of the Witch...........89

    Greater Love Has No One Than This....................92

CHAPTER FIFTEEN: Deeper Magic from Before the Dawn
    of Time..95

    The Lion Roars...100

CHAPTER SIXTEEN: What Happened About the Statues..103

CHAPTER SEVENTEEN: The Hunting of the White Stag..107

Does He Know? Do You?...111

Continuing the Adventure..114

    Tea with Mr. Tumnus 114

    Edmund's Turkish Delight 117

    Make the Story Your Own 118

    Read the Other Books in the Series 119

    A List of Main Characters.................................122

    Map of Narnia..125

    Find Out More..126

WELCOME TO NARNIA: AN INTRODUCTION

The Lion, the Witch and the Wardrobe—I was seven years old when I was given my first copy. Little did I know that it would have a profound and lasting impact on my life. I quickly devoured the rest of the Narnia series—*The Magician's Nephew, Prince Caspian, The Horse and His Boy, The Voyage of the Dawn Treader, The Silver Chair, The Last Battle.*

As a child, I read each of the books more than a dozen times, until they literally fell apart. Every time I read them, I enjoyed them more. And I discovered, as millions of others have, that there is far more to *The Chronicles of Narnia* than meets the eye. There are stories within the stories. *The*

Chronicles of Narnia are full of hidden truths, deep mysteries, and spiritual treasures.

C. S. Lewis insisted that *The Chronicles* are not allegories, though many people have described them as such. Technically speaking, this is true. In an allegory, every character and event is a symbol of something else. Many of the characters and events in Narnia do not represent anything in particular—they are simply elements of the wonderful and fantastic adventures Lewis created. But many characters and events do represent something else, something from the spiritual realm. And although Lewis did not initially intend to write stories that would illustrate the most vital truths of the Christian faith, that is essentially what he did.

Jesus said, "Out of the abundance of the heart the mouth speaks" (Matthew 12:34, ESV). Consciously and perhaps at times even unconsciously, Lewis wound powerful biblical truths through every chapter, every scene in *The Chronicles*. His deeply rooted faith naturally found its expression in everything he wrote.

In *The Voyage of the Dawn Treader* (Book 5), the great Lion Aslan tells the two Pevensie children that their adventures in Narnia have come to an end: They will not be returning to this country again. Edmund and Lucy are horribly upset.

"It isn't Narnia, you know," sobbed Lucy. "It's you. We shan't meet you there. And how can we live, never meeting you?"

"But you shall meet me, dear one," said Aslan.

"Are—are you there too, Sir?" said Edmund.
"I am," said Aslan. "But there I have another name. You must learn to know me by that name. This was the very reason why you were brought to Narnia, that by knowing me here for a little, you may know me better there."

Years ago, after reading this passage in *Dawn Treader*, a little girl named Hila wrote to C. S. Lewis, asking him to tell her Aslan's other name. Lewis responded, "Well, I want you to guess. Has there ever been anyone in this world who 1) arrived at the same time as Father Christmas, 2) Said he was the son of the Great Emperor, 3) Gave himself up for someone else's fault to be jeered at and killed by wicked people, 4) Came to life again, 5) Is sometimes spoken of as a lamb (see the end of *Dawn Treader*). Don't you really know His name in this world? Think it over and let me know your answer."

Just as Edmund and Lucy's adventures in Narnia helped them come to know Aslan (Jesus) better, our adventures in Narnia can do the same for us. But sometimes, like little Hila, we may miss the deeper truths behind the stories. This book is written to help readers identify and understand some of the many spiritual treasures in *The Lion, the Witch and the Wardrobe.*

It begins with an introduction to the creator of Narnia, C. S. Lewis. As you read about the life and times of this extraordinary man, you'll find that many of the details of his stories take on a new and special significance. Then "Step into the Wardrobe" to learn more about the book that started it all—*The Lion, the Witch and the Wardrobe.* (It became "Book Two" when the prequel, *The Magician's Nephew,* was released. At Lewis's suggestion, the publishers later renumbered the series to reflect the chronology of the stories themselves rather than the publication date.)

"The Story Within the Story" takes you through *The Lion, the Witch and the Wardrobe* chapter by chapter—highlighting the spiritual truths and scriptural symbolism. This section is meant to be read side by side with the original book. For every chapter you will find a key verse that reflects one of the primary spiritual themes. You'll also find a list of biblical parallels and principles. In some cases it shows which events in Narnia are similar or even identical to stories in the Bible. In other cases it indicates where a particular element of Lewis's story illustrates an important scriptural principle. Each chapter in that section of the book concludes with an interesting fact or point to ponder and some additional Scriptures you can read, related to a previously mentioned topic. You'll also find a series of reflections or meditations throughout that develop and expand on the biblical truths.

Parents, grandparents, and teachers who are reading along with their children or grandchildren or students may want to use the material to help start thoughtful discussion or extend story time into Scripture reading and family devotions. If you plan to use the book this way, it would be best not to attempt to cover all of the material offered in each and every chapter. Instead, choose one or two points that seem most interesting and meaningful to you, and go from there.

"Continuing the Adventure," you'll discover how to have a real English tea party, as Lucy did with Mr. Tumnus. Make your own Turkish Delight, and taste the treat that Edmund found so tempting. Find ways to express your thoughts and feelings about the story. And learn more about the wonderful adventures that await you in the other books in *The Chronicles of Narnia*.

It is my hope and prayer that this book will help those who want to gain a deeper understanding and appreciation of *The Lion, the Witch and the Wardrobe*. And that having read this book, you will love the original all the more. Ultimately, may you find yourself developing an even deeper love for the source of Lewis's inspiration: the Word of God.

—CHRISTIN DITCHFIELD

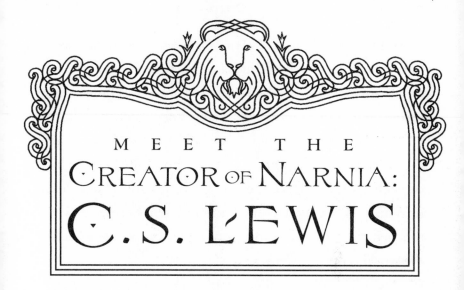

MEET THE CREATOR OF NARNIA: C. S. LEWIS

When his mother told him that he was going to meet the famous author C. S. Lewis, eight-year-old Douglas Gresham could hardly contain himself. *The Chronicles of Narnia* were among his favorite bedtime stories, and now he was about to be introduced to their creator.

As they walked through the door of Mr. Lewis's cottage, called The Kilns, Douglas heard a big, booming voice welcoming them: "Aha! Here they are. Here they are!"

Before them stood a slightly stooped, balding gentleman in baggy trousers and a rumpled tweed jacket, with the elbows worn away. His teeth were yellowish, and his large face was rather red, though alive with warmth and expression.

At first Douglas was terribly disappointed: "Here was a man who was on speaking terms with King Peter, with the

Great Lion, Aslan himself. Here was the man who had been to Narnia; surely he should at least wear silver chain mail and be girt about with a jewel-encrusted sword-belt. This was the heroic figure of whom Mother had so often spoken?"

But Douglas's disappointment did not last long. Over the years, as he got to know the man who would become his stepfather, he discovered him to be every bit the hero he had imagined—a funny, clever, kind, and generous man who touched the hearts and minds of countless people around the world.

According to a recent estimate, C. S. Lewis's books have been translated into more than thirty languages and have sold over two hundred million copies worldwide. He is routinely quoted by preachers and professors, presidents and prime ministers. Many of the most prominent leaders of the Christian faith today readily acknowledge having been profoundly influenced by Lewis and his writings.

Clive Staples Lewis was born on November 29, 1898, in Belfast, Northern Ireland. He never did like his name. When he was barely four years old, the precocious little boy announced to the family that his name was Jacksie—and he absolutely refused to answer to anything else. So from then on, that's what everyone called him: Jacksie or Jacks. And later on, just Jack. Jack's older brother Warren—whom he nicknamed Warnie—was his constant companion and closest friend. The two boys spent hours exploring the gardens and forests and fields around their country home. On rainy days they climbed up into an old wardrobe and told each other stories about talking animals, magic kingdoms, and the knights and dragons that inhabited faraway lands.

When Warnie was sent away to boarding school, Jack was very lonely. He had to find new ways to spend his time. "My father bought all the books he read and never got rid of any of them," Jack said. "In the seemingly endless afternoons I took volume after volume from the shelves." Jack was allowed to read whatever he wanted, and he chose some very grown-up books: histories, biographies, books of poetry written in Latin and French. But some of his favorites were the children's stories written by Edith Nesbit and Beatrix Potter.

It wasn't long before Jack began writing poems, plays, and stories of his own. "I wrote about chivalrous mice and rabbits who rode out in complete mail to kill not giants but cats," he later recalled. Jack illustrated his work with drawings of important characters and scenes or detailed maps of the lands in which they lived. Warnie could hardly wait to get home during the holidays to see what Jack had done— and Jack could hardly wait to show him.

Albert Lewis, the boys' father, was a kind but distant man—consumed with the pressures of work and the demands of his career. Jack was only nine when their beloved mother, Flora, was diagnosed with cancer. The thought of losing her terrified Jack. He fervently prayed for a miracle, pleading with God to heal his mother. But Flora did not get better. In fact, not long afterward she died. Albert fell into a deep depression. His two young sons felt abandoned and alone. It seemed to Jack as if "all settled happiness, all that was tranquil and reliable, disappeared from my life." Believing he had been betrayed, Jack turned his back on God completely.

Soon after, Jack was sent off to boarding school. It was, for the most part, a miserable experience. Nearly all of his classes emphasized math skills, which Jack wasn't particularly good at and didn't like. His classmates were cruel, his teachers were insensitive and unkind, and the principal of the school was literally losing his mind. Eventually Albert realized that his youngest son would do better in a different environment. He sent Jack to study with a private tutor. It was Professor Kirkpatrick who discovered that Jack was a brilliant student with a special gift for language and literature. He greatly encouraged Jack in his studies.

As a teenager, Jack was still very bitter over his mother's death. He delved deeper and deeper into the world of academia, dismissing God and religion and the teachings of the church as foolishness. At the same time he was desperately searching for something to fill the emptiness—the longing—deep within him. "I was at this time living, like so many atheists and anti-theists, in a whirl of contradictions. I maintained that God did not exist. I was also very angry with God for not existing."

At the age of eighteen, Lewis received a scholarship to the prestigious University College at Oxford. He was not long in the classroom, however, before duty called him to enlist in the armed forces. World War I had begun, and Jack was sent to the front lines in France. Wounded in battle, he returned home less than a year later. But the horrors of war would stay with him all of his life.

Eventually Lewis completed his education and became a college professor, teaching Medieval and Renaissance Literature at Oxford. He published several volumes of poetry and was well on his way to being recognized as a distinguished scholar and literary critic. Yet his intellectual and academic accomplishments did little to quell the turmoil within. In the stimulating environment of the university, surrounded by some of the greatest minds in the world, Lewis couldn't help but recognize the contradictory and illogical nature of his unbelief.

"My argument against God was that the universe seemed so cruel and unjust. But how had I got this idea of just and unjust? A man does not call a line crooked unless he has some idea of a straight line."

For some time Lewis fought hard to hold on to his atheistic worldview. He engaged in heated intellectual debates with other professors who were devout Christians, most notably fellow author J. R. R. Tolkien (*The Lord of the Rings*). Over time, in spite of himself, Lewis began to see that there were answers—logical, intelligent answers—to his most critical questions. In the language he could relate to, using mythological, philosophical, and theological illustrations he was familiar with, these friends and coworkers challenged Lewis to rethink his beliefs. They helped him grasp the reality of the faith that had confounded him.

Finally, at the age of thirty-one, Jack could not hide behind his flawed and empty arguments anymore. "I gave in and admitted that God was God, and knelt and prayed; perhaps, that night, the most dejected and reluctant convert in all England." His conversion from avowed atheist to committed Christian was not an overnight event. In fact, it was a lengthy process that took place in steps and stages as he came to terms with divine truth on a profoundly intellectual level. But in the end, it dawned on him as quietly, as gently, as surely as a sunrise.

"I know very well when, but hardly how, the final step was taken," Lewis once said. "I was driven to Whipsnade one sunny morning. When we set out I did not believe that Jesus Christ is the Son of God, and when we reached the zoo I did. Yet I had not exactly spent the journey in thought. Nor in great emotion."

Somehow as simply as that, the battle for Jack's heart and mind was over. He surrendered himself completely to the Lordship of Christ. Much later Lewis would write a spiritual autobiography that detailed his journey to faith.

He called it *Surprised by Joy.* For as a Christian, he did find the joy and peace and hope that had eluded him in his youth. He would go on to become the greatest Christian apologist of the century. With his genius, Lewis could convincingly articulate the case for Christianity like no one ever had—ably defending the faith and refuting the arguments of the most clever atheists and agnostics. With crystal clarity, he explained some of the most complicated concepts in Scripture, those that had baffled and befuddled theologians for ages. Lewis's approach was so effective—he led so many members of the intellectual and academic community to faith in Christ—that the media dubbed him "the apostle to the skeptics."

During World War II Lewis addressed matters of faith in a series of radio programs broadcast all over England. These talks were collected and compiled into a book entitled *Mere Christianity.* This was followed by *The Problem of Pain* and *The Screwtape Letters.* By now Lewis had achieved worldwide fame. A popular speaker as well as a best-selling author, he was featured in hundreds of magazine and newspaper articles. He participated in numerous lectures and debates on university campuses.

While teaching at Oxford and later Cambridge, Lewis continued to write books on literary criticism. He experimented with a science fiction trilogy. And drawing on the fantastic stories and imaginary worlds he had invented as a child, he completed a series of seven books for children he called *The Chronicles of Narnia*.

Today Lewis's fairy tales are widely regarded as classic literature, consistently ranked among the greatest children's books ever written. Children everywhere have immediately recognized what Lewis called the "stories within the stories." They have correctly identified the central character—the Great Lion Aslan—as a beautiful representation of Jesus Christ. With *The Chronicles of Narnia*, Lewis has helped generations of children to understand the powerful, life-changing truths of the Bible in a whole new way.

Lewis never had any children of his own. He remained a bachelor until the age of fifty-eight, when he was once again "surprised by Joy." That is, he met and married American writer Joy Davidman. Sadly, their happiness did not last long—Joy died of cancer only four years later. Lewis helped raise her two sons, Douglas and David. He kept a journal vividly describing the pain and suffering he endured at his wife's passing *(A Grief Observed)*. Though he felt the same hurt and anger and bitterness he had experienced after the loss of his mother, this time Lewis did not turn away from God. Instead he turned to Him and found the strength to carry on. His faith grew even stronger as he experienced God's mercy and grace in a whole new way.

Lewis kept busy writing and speaking and—with help from his brother Warnie—answering each one of the thousands of letters he received from fans around the globe.

On November 22, 1963, the world was reeling over the assassination of President John F. Kennedy. That same day, after a long illness, C. S. Lewis passed away. In an instant he found himself in the presence of the God he had once tried so hard to escape. The God whose love finally overwhelmed him and completely conquered his resistance. The God who humbled him and surprised him with joy.

STEP INTO THE
WARDROBE

It began with a picture in his head—a picture of a faun carrying an umbrella and parcels in a snowy wood. C. S. Lewis was only sixteen at the time. But more than thirty years later, he still remembered the scene he had vividly imagined. By this time Lewis had become a world-famous author and lecturer. One day he decided he would try to write a story about the picture. As he thought about it, other pictures began to appear in his mind's eye: a queen on a sledge and a magnificent lion.

"Suddenly Aslan came bounding in," Lewis later explained. "I don't know where the Lion came from or why He came. But once He was there, He pulled the whole story together."

As he sat down to write the book that would become *The Lion, the Witch and the Wardrobe,* Lewis drew from many of his own real-life experiences. He recalled how he and his brother Warnie used to climb up into an old wardrobe and tell each other stories about talking animals, magic kingdoms, knights, and dragons. Much later a little girl visiting Lewis's home asked him if there was anything behind the wardrobe he still kept there. Perhaps there was, Lewis thought. What if other worlds really did exist and you could get to them by stepping into a wardrobe? Lewis let his imagination soar.

A number of children had recently come to stay with Jack and Warnie and their housekeeper, Mrs. Moore. It was during World War II, and German fighter planes were conducting air raids against Great Britain. They dropped thousands of bombs on the most heavily populated cities. Whenever possible, parents sent their children to live with friends and relatives out in the country, where it was safer.

Of course, Lewis had no children of his own, and he hadn't really spent any time with young people in years. But as he got to know the children who stayed in his home, Lewis discovered something that alarmed him. These children didn't seem to know how to entertain themselves. They didn't have much imagination at all. They didn't read. And they were in way too much of a hurry to become adults. These children didn't have any time for things they considered "baby-ish."

Lewis understood. He had felt that way once—but he knew better now.

"When I was ten, I read fairy tales in secret and would have been ashamed if I had been found doing so," he admitted. "Now that I am fifty, I read them openly. When I became a man I put away childish things, including the fear of childishness and the desire to be very grown-up."

Lewis thought of all the wonderful stories he had loved to read as a child and how they had impacted his life. It made him sad to think what the children of his day were missing. Yet there weren't many contemporary books he could recommend to them—books that would not merely educate but encourage and inspire them. It was all the more reason Lewis should write stories of his own. "People won't write the books I want, so I have to do it for myself," he concluded.

Lewis's first children's book began with the sentence, "Once there were four children whose names were Peter, Susan, Edmund and Lucy."

Peter was the name of the talking-mouse hero of all the stories he had written as a boy. Lucy was the daughter of Lewis's good friend, Owen Barfield. In addition to naming one of the main characters after her, Lewis decided to dedicate the book to her as well:

My Dear Lucy,
I wrote this story for you, but when I began it I had not realized that girls grow quicker than books. As a result you are already too old for fairy tales, and by the time it is printed and

bound you will be older still. But some day you will be old enough to start reading fairy tales again. You can then take it down from some upper shelf, dust it and tell me what you think of it. I shall probably be too deaf to hear, and too old to understand a word you say, but I shall still be

your affectionate Godfather,
C. S. Lewis

In *The Lion, the Witch and the Wardrobe,* the four children are sent to stay at the country home of Professor Kirke. Lewis named the professor for his old tutor, W. T. Kirkpatrick. Kirkpatrick was a gruff but kindhearted man who always insisted his students must learn to use "logic" to carefully think things through. Of course in some ways the character of Professor Kirke was not unlike C. S. Lewis, who had become a professor himself.

While exploring the professor's rambling country home, the children climb into a wardrobe to hide from the no-nonsense housekeeper, Mrs. Macready (Mrs. Moore). Inside the wardrobe, the children discover the magical world of Narnia.

As Lewis created Narnia, he drew on all the imaginary worlds described by the children's authors he loved—Edith Nesbit, Beatrix Potter, and George MacDonald, whom Lewis considered a "master" of fantasy and fairy tale. Lewis filled his own world with all the creatures from his favorite fairy tales and legends. He added bits and pieces from his studies of Roman, Greek, and Hebrew mythology, as well as from medieval literature. And then suddenly he was inspired to weave into the story something infinitely more precious to him—his Christian faith. Through Aslan, Lewis would introduce his readers to the character and person of Jesus Christ—the Son of God, who willingly laid down His life for sinners and rose from the dead in power and glory. (The name "Aslan" comes from the Turkish word for "lion," and in the Bible, Jesus is sometimes referred to as "the Lion of the tribe of Judah.")

Every week C. S. Lewis met with a group of professors, poets, and philosophers—all of them authors like himself. They called themselves the Inklings. At each meeting, members took turns sharing with each other what they had written. The group then discussed and debated various points. They offered both praise and constructive criticism. One of Lewis's closest friends was fellow Inkling J. R. R. Tolkien. Tolkien had recently published *The Hobbit*, and he was about to complete *The Lord of the Rings*.

The two men shared a love of myth and legend, but they had a very different approach to writing their own fairy tales. Although he, too, was a devout Christian, Tolkien preferred to avoid including any kind of spiritual or allegorical elements in his stories. Tolkien had spent nearly thirteen years painstakingly creating the world of Middle-Earth, complete with hundreds of pages of history and geography as background material. The languages he invented were presented in such detail that they could actually be studied and learned. It seemed to Tolkien that Lewis had dashed off his story in a rush, without taking time to properly develop it. Furthermore, Tolkien thought it was inappropriate to combine characters from the mythology of different cultures and eras—as Lewis did when he included the contemporary British Father Christmas in a story that also featured the ancient Roman god of wine, Bacchus.

At first Lewis was stung by his friend's criticism. They remained good friends, of course. But Tolkien's opinion meant so much to Lewis that he seriously considered abandoning the whole idea of writing a children's book.

Fortunately Lewis got up the nerve to read his work to another friend, Roger Lancelyn Green. "Do you think it's worth going on with?" Lewis asked him.

Green's response was the opposite of Tolkien's. "As he read, there had crept over me a feeling of awe and excitement," Green later said. "Not only that it was better than most children's books which were appearing at the time—but the conviction that I was listening to the first reading of a great classic."

The Lion, the Witch and the Wardrobe was published in 1950. Just as Green had predicted, it became an instant classic—a perennial best-seller. Over the next five years,

Lewis wrote six more books in the series that would become known as *The Chronicles of Narnia*. Today millions of readers in countries all over the globe have discovered the power of inspiration and imagination as they've stepped into the wardrobe and explored the wonderful world of Narnia.

"THE STORY WITHIN THE STORY"

*In reality however he [Aslan] is an invention giving
an imaginary answer to the question, "What might Christ
become like, if there really were a world like Narnia
and He chose to be incarnate and die and
rise again in that world as He has actually done in ours?"*

C. S. LEWIS

This is the premise of the very first book about Narnia—the most famous and beloved book in *The Chronicles*—the one that started it all: *The Lion, the Witch and the Wardrobe.*

The adventure begins when Peter, Susan, Edmund, and Lucy tumble through the door of a mysterious wardrobe into Narnia—an enchanted world of talking beasts, fauns, dwarfs, giants, and other wonderful creatures. The children discover that Narnia is a land in bondage—held captive for a hundred years under the spell of the evil White Witch. "It's she that makes it always winter; always winter, and never Christmas!"

Prophecies have foretold the end of the Witch's reign. One day Aslan will return to Narnia. Aslan is the Great Lion, the King of Beasts, Son of the Emperor-Beyond-the-Sea.

"Wrong will be right, when Aslan comes in sight,
At the sound of his roar, sorrows will be no more,
When he bares his teeth, winter meets its death,
And when he shakes his mane, we shall have spring again."

Furthermore, as the saying goes, two "Sons of Adam" and two "Daughters of Eve" will one day sit on the four thrones at Cair Paravel and will rule as Kings and Queens in Narnia. Now that the four children are here, could it be that Narnia's deliverance is at hand?

Over the years, millions of readers have thrilled to discover "the story within the story" of *The Lion, the Witch and the Wardrobe*. It's the story of the gospel—the story of salvation. In a general sense, all of Narnia awaits deliverance from the dominion of the White Witch. The land itself longs to be free from captivity—to return to the peace and joy and beauty of the life it once knew. "The creation waits in eager expectation for the sons of God to be revealed . . . in hope that [it] . . . will be liberated from its bondage to decay and brought into the glorious freedom of the children of God" (Romans 8:19-21).

It is also a story of personal salvation—and the personal sacrifice that makes that salvation possible. Edmund falls under the spell of the White Witch. He succumbs to his own pride, selfishness, greed, and lust. He becomes a traitor. And according to the Deep Magic (or law) on which Narnia was founded, Edmund must pay the penalty with his life. "The wages of sin is death" (Romans 6:23). "Without the shedding of blood there is no forgiveness of sins" (Hebrews 9:22, ESV).

The only hope for Narnia and for Edmund is Aslan. Only Aslan—the one who created Narnia—can now deliver it from the power of the White Witch. "The reason the Son of God appeared was to destroy the devil's work" (1 John 3:8). And it is Aslan who will lay down his own life for Edmund, taking Edmund's punishment and dying in his place. "God demonstrates his own love for us in this: While we were still sinners, Christ died for us" (Romans 5:8). Ultimately, it is in dying a torturous and agonizing death at the hands of the Witch that Aslan sets Narnia and Edmund free. For there is an even "Deeper Magic"—a greater law—at work:

> When a willing victim who had committed no treachery was killed in a traitor's stead, the Table would crack and Death itself would start working backward.

With Aslan's sacrifice on the Stone Table, the power of sin and death is broken. Aslan's resurrection marks the beginning of the Golden Age of Narnia—a time of unprecedented joy, peace, and prosperity.

The Bible tells us that "Christ redeemed us from the curse of the law" (Galatians 3:13) and that God "has rescued us from the dominion of darkness and brought us into the kingdom of the Son he loves, in whom we have redemption, the forgiveness of sins" (Colossians 1:13-14).

In addition to the themes of salvation, redemption, restoration, and reconciliation, *The Lion, the Witch and the Wardrobe* also includes illustrations of the wickedness and deceitfulness of the enemy of our souls (John 8:44). It reveals the power of sin—and its consequences (James 1:14-15). It challenges us to maintain a holy fear of and reverence for God, who is both good and terrible at the same time (Deuteronomy 7:21; Psalm 99:3).

These are just a few of the spiritual treasures you will discover as you begin your own adventure with *The Lion, the Witch and the Wardrobe!*

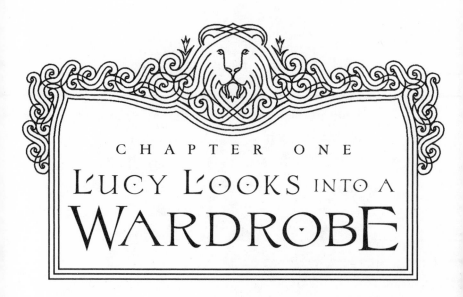

CHAPTER ONE
L·UCY L·OOKS INTO A WARDROBE

Be happy. . . . while you are young. . . .
Follow the ways of your heart and whatever your eyes see.

<small>ECCLESIASTES 11:9</small>

BIBLICAL PARALLELS AND PRINCIPLES

~ Lucy discovers that there is much more to the mysterious wardrobe than meets the eye. Jesus told His disciples not to judge things by their appearances (John 7:24). The Bible frequently refers to the discovery of hidden truths and treasures—the revelation of mysteries: "The secret things belong to the LORD our God" (Deuteronomy 29:29). "He reveals deep and hidden things" (Daniel 2:22). "It is the glory of

God has filled the world with mysteries for us
to uncover and treasures that are ours to discover.

God to conceal a matter; to search out a matter is the glory of kings" (Proverbs 25:2).

~ Twice Lewis mentions that Lucy has left the door open "because she knew that it is a very foolish thing to shut oneself into any wardrobe." The Scriptures often remind us of the value of wisdom and caution: "A prudent man gives thought to his steps" (Proverbs 14:15b; see also Proverbs 14:8, 16).

DO YOU KNOW?

Lucy is drawn further and further into the wardrobe by the light from the lamp-post. What does the Scripture call a "lamp"? And who is the "light"? (Hint: Read Psalm 119:105 and John 8:12.)

SCRIPTURES ON SEARCHING OUT THE SECRET THINGS OF GOD

1 Corinthians 2:7-13
Romans 11:33-36
Colossians 2:2-3

*Because of sin, it is both a blessing and
a curse to be a Son of Adam or a Daughter of Eve.*

CHAPTER TWO

WHAT LUCY FOUND THERE

With his mouth each speaks cordially to his neighbor,
but in his heart he sets a trap for him.

JEREMIAH 9:8B

BIBLICAL PARALLELS AND PRINCIPLES

~ When Lucy agrees to have tea with Tumnus, she walks right into a trap. The psalmist often prayed for protection from his enemies: "Keep me from the snares they have laid for me" (Psalm 141:9; see also Psalm 59:1-4; 119:86; 143:9). He asked God to expose their evil schemes—and drew comfort from the assurance that "the LORD watches over all who love him" (Psalm 145:20; see also Psalm 34:17; 40:1-2; 121).

~ Tumnus suddenly feels the weight of the sin he is committing. "My guilt has overwhelmed me like a burden too heavy to bear" (Psalm 38:4). In spite of his initial response, he realizes that it is not too late—he can still do what is right. Second Corinthians 7:10 tells us, "Godly sorrow brings repentance that leads to salvation and leaves no regret." Acts 3:19 urges, "Repent, then, and turn to God so that your sins may be wiped out, that times of refreshing may come from the Lord."

DID YOU NOTICE?

Mr. Tumnus refers to Lucy as a "Daughter of Eve." According to the Bible, all human beings are physically descended from Adam and Eve. (Genesis 3:20 tells us that Eve is "the mother of all the living.") We are also spiritually descended from Adam and Eve, in that every one of us suffers under the curse of Eden (Genesis 3:14-19). We have inherited from our first parents a sinful nature—and now, like them, we are in need of a Savior (Romans 5:12-19).

SCRIPTURES ON TRUE REPENTANCE

- Joel 2:12-13
- Psalm 51
- 1 John 1:9

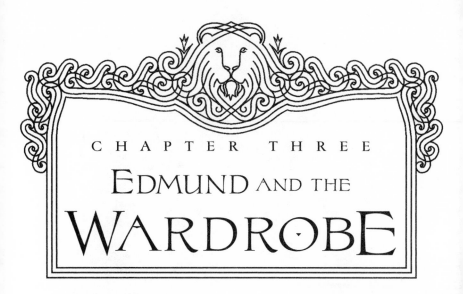

CHAPTER THREE

EDMUND AND THE
WARDROBE

A man who lacks judgment derides his neighbor,
but a man of understanding holds his tongue.

PROVERBS 11:12

BIBLICAL PARALLELS AND PRINCIPLES

~ As a brother, Edmund proves to be mean-spirited, selfish, and unkind. He delights in mocking Lucy and looks for ways to provoke her. Proverbs 17:19 says, "He who loves a quarrel loves sin." Proverbs 18:21 cautions, "The tongue has the power of life and death, and those who love it will eat its fruit." Colossians 3:12 tells us how we should behave: "Clothe yourselves with compassion, kindness, humility,

Appearances can be deceiving.

gentleness and patience." First Thessalonians 5:15 says, "Always try to be kind to each other."

~ In many fairy tales a white witch is a good witch, and white magic is good magic—as opposed to "evil," "dark," or "black" magic. But in *The Lion, the Witch and the Wardrobe*, C. S. Lewis uses white to represent winter and death. It paints a picture of a world that is cold and colorless. For in Narnia—and in the Scriptures—there's no such thing as a "good witch." Deuteronomy 18:10-12 warns, "Let no one be found among you who . . . practices divination or sorcery, interprets omens, engages in witchcraft, or casts spells, or who is a medium or spiritist or who consults the dead. Anyone who does these things is detestable to the LORD."

DO YOU KNOW?

Lucy is telling the truth, but Edmund doesn't believe her story about the wardrobe. The Bible tells us about Someone whose brothers and sisters didn't believe what He said either. Do you know who? (Hint: Read John 7:3-5.)

SCRIPTURES ON BROTHERLY LOVE

- John 13:34-35
- 1 Peter 3:8
- 1 Corinthians 13

Greed is a dangerous thing.

CHAPTER FOUR

TURKISH DELIGHT

Stolen water is sweet; food eaten in secret is delicious!

PROVERBS 9:17

BIBLICAL PARALLELS AND PRINCIPLES

~ The White Witch suddenly changes her tone with Edmund and represents herself as a friend. But 1 John 3:7 says, "Dear children, do not let anyone lead you astray." Second Corinthians 11:14-15 explains, "Satan himself masquerades as an angel of light . . . his servants masquerade as servants of righteousness." And "by appealing to the lustful desires of sinful human nature, they entice people" (2 Peter 2:18). "By smooth talk and flattery they deceive the minds of naive people" (Romans 16:18b).

~ Edmund's greed gets the better of his judgment. Proverbs 23:1-3 cautions, "When you sit to dine with a ruler, note well what is before you, and put a knife to your throat if you are given to gluttony. Do not crave his delicacies, for that food is deceptive."

THINK ABOUT IT!

The Bible tells us repeatedly to resist temptation and instead obey God's commandments. One of the problems with sin is that—like the enchanted Turkish Delight—it's addictive. It separates us from God. James 1:14-15 explains, "Each one is tempted when, by his own evil desire, he is dragged away and enticed. Then, after desire has conceived, it gives birth to sin; and sin, when it is full-grown, gives birth to death." How does the Bible say we should handle temptation? (Hint: Read James 4:7.)

SCRIPTURES ON PURE DELIGHT

- Isaiah 61:10
- Psalm 37:4
- Zephaniah 3:17

DEADLY DELIGHT

At last the Turkish Delight was all finished and Edmund was looking
very hard at the empty box and wishing that she would ask him
whether he would like some more. Probably the Queen knew quite
well what he was thinking; for she knew, though Edmund did not,
that this was enchanted Turkish Delight and that anyone who
had once tasted it would want more and more of it, and would even,
if they were allowed, go on eating it till they killed themselves.

The Queen has found Edmund alone in the snowy
woods of Narnia. Under the guise of friendship and
compassion, she invites the shivering boy to warm himself
in her sleigh. And she gives him the most delicious food he
has ever eaten—Turkish Delight. But unbeknownst to
Edmund, this sweet, gooey candy—no matter how delicious

it tastes—is poisonous. Under its influence, he will lose any good sense or judgment he might have had. He will ignore all the hints and warnings that something is not right, that there may be a sinister side to the cold and beautiful Queen. He will lie about having met her, pretend he knows nothing about the frozen land over which she reigns, and criticize or ridicule anyone who tries to open his eyes to the truth. The Turkish Delight will take complete control of him. It's Edmund's desire for more and more of the magical food that will ultimately lead him to betray his own brother and sisters.

You know, the power of the enchanted Turkish Delight is not unlike the power of sin. It seems so appealing on the surface. It offers to bring us comfort, satisfaction, even delight. What harm can there be, we wonder, giving in to this thought or that action? Besides, we can keep it to ourselves. Who will ever know? Proverbs 9:17 observes, "Stolen water is sweet; food eaten in secret is delicious!" But as Adam and Eve discovered in the Garden of Eden, one bite really can kill you. Regardless of how sweetly he speaks to us, Satan is no friend. And the "food" he offers never brings the satisfaction it promises. Instead, it leads to our destruction.

When we give in to temptation, when we let go of wisdom and sound judgment and do what we know we should not do, it starts a chain reaction. James 1:14-15 explains, "Each one is tempted when, by his own evil desire, he is dragged away and enticed. Then, after desire has conceived, it gives birth to sin; and sin, when it is full-grown, gives birth to death."

Death. The death of our joy, the death of our peace. The death of our relationships with God and with others. And eventually, if we do not repent, the eternal death of our spirit. The biggest mistake we can make is to let down our guard, underestimate the power of sin, and close our eyes to its consequences.

The Scripture warns, "Be self-controlled and alert. Your enemy the devil prowls around . . . looking for someone to devour. Resist him, standing firm in the faith" (1 Peter 5:8-9). No matter how tempting, how delicious a sinful choice may seem, it's not worth the price we'll pay. We must learn to resist the enemy of our souls, reject his invitations, and refuse to partake of his deadly "delights."

*Sometimes it's harder
to believe the truth than a lie.*

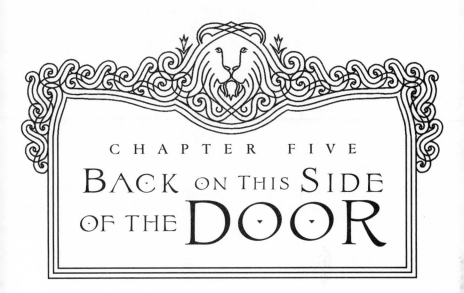

CHAPTER FIVE

BACK ON THIS SIDE OF THE DOOR

Reckless words pierce like a sword,
but the tongue of the wise brings healing.

PROVERBS 12:18

BIBLICAL PARALLELS AND PRINCIPLES

~ Edmund continues being mean and nasty to Lucy. Proverbs 11:17 warns, "A kind man benefits himself, but a cruel man brings trouble on himself."

~ Lucy refuses to change her story—she knows the truth for herself, even if no one else believes her. To those who suffer persecution and experience the temptation to take the easy way out, the Scriptures say, "Stand firm. Let nothing move you" (1 Corinthians 15:58). "Speak the truth to each other" (Zechariah 8:16), "holding on to faith and a good conscience" (1 Timothy 1:19).

~ Just as Peter and Susan were concerned about Lucy, the Bible tells us that Jesus' brothers and sisters were concerned about Him. They did not believe what He said about being the Son of God: "When his family heard about this, they went to take charge of him, for they said, 'He is out of his mind'" (Mark 3:21).

DO YOU KNOW?

Sometimes our friends and family forsake us (see Job 19:19). Edmund denied having ever been in Narnia with Lucy. When the going got tough, one of Jesus' closest disciples denied even knowing Him. Do you remember who? (Hint: Read Luke 22:54-62.)

SCRIPTURES ON BEASTLY BEHAVIOR

- Psalm 57:4
- James 4:1-3
- Galatians 5:13-15

CHAPTER SIX

INTO THE
FOREST

The path of the righteous is like the first gleam of dawn,
shining ever brighter till the full light of day.

PROVERBS 4:18

BIBLICAL PARALLELS AND PRINCIPLES

~ Though Edmund still refuses to acknowledge any wrong-doing, Peter is quick to apologize for not believing Lucy. "He who conceals his sins does not prosper, but whoever confesses and renounces them finds mercy" (Proverbs 28:13).

~ The children realize that they have a responsibility to Mr. Tumnus. He has shown compassion to Lucy. Isaiah 16:3 commands us, "Hide the fugitives, do not betray the refugees." Isaiah 1:17 says, "Seek justice, encourage the oppressed."

God calls us to help the hurting
and to rescue those in danger.

Hebrews 13:3 urges, "Remember those in prison as if you were their fellow prisoners, and those who are mistreated as if you yourselves were suffering." Proverbs 24:11 tells us, "Rescue those being led away to death."

~ Peter and Edmund debate about whether or not they can trust Tumnus and the Robin—though Edmund has already made a secret and dangerous alliance with the White Witch. Proverbs 12:26 says, "A righteous man is cautious in friendship, but the way of the wicked leads them astray."

THINK ABOUT IT!

Instead of admitting his own guilt, Edmund blames his brother and sisters for being unkind to him. He comforts himself with thoughts of revenge. How does the Bible say we should respond to those who mistreat us? (Hint: Read Matthew 5:38-44.)

SCRIPTURES ON FORGIVENESS AND RECONCILIATION

- Ephesians 4:32
- Luke 17:3-4
- Colossians 3:12-14

God has a purpose and a plan
for each of our lives.

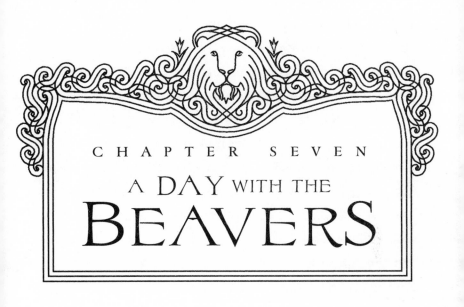

CHAPTER SEVEN

A DAY WITH THE
BEAVERS

We wait for you; your name
and renown are the desire of our hearts.

ISAIAH 26:8

BIBLICAL PARALLELS AND PRINCIPLES

~ "Aslan is on the move!" At the mention of his name, the
children have what theologians call a "numinous"—a mysterious, supernatural—experience of the divine presence. It
awakens one's spiritual understanding and elicits a profound personal response. To the righteous the name of the
Lord is "glorious and awesome" (Deuteronomy 28:58),
"majestic" (Psalm 8:1), and worthy of praise (Psalm 113:3).

To the wicked it speaks of judgment (Isaiah 64:2) and is the object of blasphemy and scorn (Psalm 139:20; Isaiah 52:5).

~ Further on, in Chapter Eight, the children learn that their arrival in Narnia is seen as the fulfillment of prophecy—a sign that Narnia's long-awaited deliverance is near. "The creation waits in eager expectation for the sons of God to be revealed" (Romans 8:19). This is why upon meeting them, Mrs. Beaver exclaims, "To think I should live to see this day!" In Luke 2:29-30, Simeon rejoiced to witness the arrival of the Christ-child, Israel's Deliverer: "Sovereign Lord, as you have promised, you now dismiss your servant in peace. For my eyes have seen your salvation."

DID YOU KNOW?

In a letter to a friend, C. S. Lewis declared that Aslan was not an allegorical figure, like those of John Bunyan's *Pilgrim's Progress*, because Lewis held to a strict literary/academic definition of the word *allegory*. Instead, he explained, Aslan "is an invention giving an imaginary answer to the question, 'What might Christ become like, if there really were a world like Narnia and He chose to be incarnate and die and rise again in that world as He has actually done in ours?'"

SCRIPTURES ON THE POWER OF JESUS' NAME

- Acts 3:6, 16
- John 18:4-6
- Philippians 2:9-11

CHAPTER EIGHT

WHAT HAPPENED AFTER DINNER

Do you not know? Have you not heard?
The LORD is the everlasting God,
the Creator of the ends of the earth.

ISAIAH 40:28

BIBLICAL PARALLELS AND PRINCIPLES

~ Aslan has many names: King, Lord, Son of the Great Emperor-Beyond-the-Sea, King of Beasts, the Great Lion. The Bible tells us that—among other things—Jesus is the King of kings and Lord of lords (Revelation 19:16), the Son of God, the Son of Man (Luke 22:69-70), and the Lion of Judah (Revelation 5:5).

~ Like the prophecies about Aslan, there are countless prophecies in the Bible about the coming of the Messiah, "the anointed one," "the Deliverer". Among them: He would set wrong to right (Isaiah 61:1-2). He would "roar like a lion" (Hosea 11:10-11; Jeremiah 25:30). He would end sorrow and suffering (Isaiah 65:19; Revelation 21:4). He would destroy the works of the devil (Psalm 110:1; 1 John 3:8; Psalm 2:7-9). He would bring new life (Haggai 2:6-7; Isaiah 55:12; John 10:10).

~ Like Aslan, the Lion of Judah is "not a tame lion." He cannot be controlled or manipulated. He doesn't exist to serve us—we exist to serve Him. Romans 11:33-34 exclaims, "Oh, the depth of the riches of the wisdom and knowledge of God! How unsearchable his judgments, and his paths beyond tracing out! Who has known the mind of the Lord? Or who has been his counselor?" His ways are not our ways (Isaiah 55:8-9). We cannot always understand what He chooses to do—or chooses not to do. But this we do know: "The LORD is good and his love endures forever; his faithfulness continues through all generations" (Psalm 100:5).

~ The White Witch has no power over Aslan—she will barely be able to stand in his presence. The Bible tells us that the demons are subject to Christ (Luke 10:17). They fall down before Him (Mark 3:11), trembling (James 2:19). Believers need not fear the evil one, "whom the Lord Jesus will overthrow with the breath of his mouth and destroy by the splendor of his coming" (2 Thessalonians 2:8).

CAN THAT BE RIGHT?

Could the Witch really be a descendant of Adam's "first wife"? Written by a literary scholar, *The Chronicles of Narnia* are not only full of biblical allusions, but also of numerous references to classical literature and ancient mythology. According to a bizarre Jewish myth—concocted many years after the Scriptures were recorded—Adam had an evil and rebellious first wife, a she-demon named Lilith. (In recent years, Lilith has become a symbolic figure for feminists, as well as for those who practice the occult or engage in perversion.) It made for an interesting explanation of the White Witch's origin in a fairy tale, but as C. S. Lewis knew well, the Bible says Adam's first and only wife was Eve (Genesis 3:20).

SCRIPTURES ON THE COMING OF THE MESSIAH

- Micah 5:2
- Isaiah 9:6-7
- Matthew 12:18-21

IS HE
SAFE?

"Is—is he a man?" asked Lucy.

"Aslan a man!" said Mr. Beaver sternly. "Certainly not.
I tell you he is the king of the wood and the son of the great
Emperor-beyond-the-Sea. Don't you know what is the King of Beasts?
Aslan is a lion—the Lion, the great Lion."

Ooh!" said Susan. "Is he—quite safe?
I shall feel rather nervous about meeting a lion."

"That you will, dearie, and no mistake," said Mrs. Beaver;
"if there's anyone who can appear before Aslan without their knees
knocking, they're either braver than most or else just silly."

"Then he isn't safe?" said Lucy.

"Safe?" said Mr. Beaver; "don't you hear what Mrs. Beaver tells you?

Who said anything about safe? 'Course he isn't safe.
But he's good. He's the king, I tell you."

M r. and Mrs. Beaver are amazed that the children don't know anything about Aslan—and that they're so slow to grasp who he is.

How do you explain God to someone who has never heard of Him, never seen Him, never experienced Him? Isaiah 40:28 asks, "Do you not know? Have you not heard? The LORD is the everlasting God, the Creator of the ends of the earth." He is the King of kings, the Lord of lords, the Lion of Judah.

But as C. S. Lewis put it, He's not a tame lion.

God isn't at all safe, the way we think of safe. He isn't Someone we can control or manipulate. He doesn't perform on command. We can't be sure when or how or even if He will choose to act in the circumstances and events of our lives.

"'My thoughts are not your thoughts, neither are your ways my ways,' declares the LORD. 'As the heavens are higher than the earth, so are my ways higher than your ways and my thoughts than your thoughts'" (Isaiah 55:8-9).

The truth is that God has the right to do as He pleases. He has total control, complete authority over His creation. "The earth is the LORD's, and everything in it, the world, and all who live in it" (Psalm 24:1). He is the Sovereign Lord, Master of the Universe. Over and over the Bible tells us we must approach God in "fear and trembling"—with a holy reverence and respect. So much of who He is and what He does is beyond our comprehension.

But the Scriptures also assure us over and over again that God is good, that He is as merciful and gracious as he is just and true. "The LORD is righteous in all his ways and loving toward all he has made" (Psalm 145:17).

He has promised that He will be with us always. He will never abandon us or forsake us. When we call on Him, He will give us the strength and courage and wisdom we need to face each day. Because in everything that happens to us, He is working for our good.

"'For I know the plans I have for you,' declares the LORD, 'plans to prosper you and not to harm you, plans to give you a hope and a future'" (Jeremiah 29:11).

No, God isn't "safe." But we are safe in His care.

*We all must take sides
in the battle between good and evil.*

CHAPTER NINE

IN THE WITCH'S HOUSE

Those who live according to the sinful nature
have their minds set on what that nature desires.

ROMANS 8:5

BIBLICAL PARALLELS AND PRINCIPLES

~ Edmund's reaction to the name of Aslan is one of fear and horror. Romans 8:7 says, "The sinful mind is hostile to God." First John 1:5 tells us that "God is light," and as John 3:20 explains, "Everyone who does evil hates the light, and will not come into the light for fear his deeds will be exposed."

~ Although deep down he knows better than to trust the White Witch, Edmund cannot resist the lure of Turkish Delight. "A man is a slave to whatever has mastered him"

(2 Peter 2:19). Edmund has the opportunity to turn back, but instead he hardens his heart (Proverbs 28:14) and plunges deeper into sin (Romans 2:5).

~ The Chief of the Witch's Secret Police refers to Edmund as the "fortunate favorite of the Queen—or else not so fortunate." There is no safety or security for those who make deals with the devil. The Bible tells us he is "a liar and the father of lies" (John 8:44). He promises the world (Matthew 4:8-9), but he devours all who fall into his trap (1 Peter 5:8).

DO YOU KNOW?

In the battle of good versus evil, everyone is forced to choose sides and take a stand. Jesus told His disciples that they would face great danger because of Him: "You will be betrayed by parents, brothers, relatives and friends" (Luke 21:16). One of Jesus' closest disciples became a traitor and betrayed Him to His enemies. Do you know who? (Hint: Read Luke 22:3-6.)

SCRIPTURES ON ESCAPING FROM THE DEVIL'S TRAP

- 2 Timothy 2:22-26
- 1 Peter 5:5-9
- Galatians 5:16, 19-25

THE PATH WE CHOOSE

*It was pretty bad when he reached the far side. It was growing
darker every minute and what with that and the snowflakes swirling
all round him he could hardly see three feet ahead.
And then too there was no road. He kept slipping into deep drifts
of snow, and skidding on frozen puddles, and tripping over
fallen tree-trunks, and sliding down steep banks, and barking his shins
against rocks, till he was wet and cold and bruised all over.
The silence and the loneliness were dreadful. In fact I really think he
might have given up the whole plan and gone back and owned
up and made friends with others, if he hadn't happened to say
to himself, "When I'm King of Narnia the first thing
I shall do will be to make some decent roads."*

Deep down, Edmund knew he deserved his brother's and sisters' reproach. He had been cruel to Lucy, and he had lied to all of them. He also knew that it was wrong to take sides with the White Witch. He had set himself on a dangerous—even deadly—path. But on the way to the Witch's House he had the opportunity to rethink his decision, reconsider his course. It wasn't too late for him to admit that he was wrong and go back and make things right.

Mr. Tumnus had faced the same choice earlier on. When the faun first met Lucy in the forest, he meant to kidnap her and turn her over to the Witch. But then—like the psalmist in the Bible—he felt the weight of the sin he was committing: "My guilt has overwhelmed me like a burden too heavy to bear" (Psalm 38:4). Second Corinthians 7:10 observes, "Godly sorrow brings repentance that leads to salvation and leaves no regret."

Although he had started out on one path, Mr. Tumnus abruptly changed direction. He repented—he turned back—and he chose to do what was right.

We all make dozens of choices every day. Some of our decisions are relatively unimportant or insignificant, while others are truly life-changing. Those critical decisions take us down a particular path. Sometimes the path we've chosen is a good one. Sometimes it's not. When we realize that one of our choices was a bad one—that we're headed in the wrong direction—we're forced to make a pivotal decision.

We must choose whether or not we will continue down that path. "Sin is crouching at your door; it desires to have you, but you must master it" (Genesis 4:7).

Sometimes it seems as though it's too late. We've gone too far to turn back—we don't really have a choice. But that's not true. We always have a choice. We can blind ourselves to the truth, harden our hearts as Edmund did, and go from bad to worse. Or we can open our eyes, humble our hearts as Mr. Tumnus did, and take steps to make things right. Acts 3:19 urges us, "Repent, then, and turn to God, so that your sins may be wiped out, that times of refreshing may come from the Lord."

One path leads to even greater sin, guilt, and despair. The other leads to forgiveness, healing, and hope. The choice is up to us.

Each one of us has been given
our own special gifts and talents.

CHAPTER TEN

THE SPELL BEGINS TO BREAK

How beautiful on the mountains are the feet of those
who bring good news, who proclaim peace, who bring good tidings,
who proclaim salvation, who say to Zion, "Your God reigns."

ISAIAH 52:7

BIBLICAL PARALLELS AND PRINCIPLES

~ The others find Mrs. Beaver's careful and methodical preparations exasperating. But Proverbs 14:15 tells us, "A prudent man gives thought to his steps." Proverbs 19:2 advises, "It is not good to have zeal without knowledge, nor to be hasty and miss the way."

~ Father Christmas brings each of the children gifts. These gifts are "tools not toys"—tools that will help them fulfill their calling and face the challenges that lie ahead. According to the Scriptures, Jesus sent the Holy Spirit to give believers spiritual gifts for the same purpose. The Spirit gives these gifts "to each man [and woman], just as he determines" (1 Corinthians 12:11; compare vv. 4-31). Some are given gifts of leadership; others are given gifts of faith, wisdom, and discernment. Some have "gifts of healing" and the ability to help others (1 Corinthians 12:28). Each believer is a part of "the body of Christ" (1 Corinthians 12:27). And each one has his or her own special gift and calling (1 Corinthians 12:18).

THINK ABOUT IT!

Children often wrote to C. S. Lewis to ask him about Aslan's true identity—his other name in our world. Lewis always answered by giving hints, including this one: "Who in our world arrived at the same time as Father Christmas?" (Hint: Read Luke 2:1-20.)

SCRIPTURES ON THE WEAPONS OF SPIRITUAL WARFARE

- Ephesians 6:10-18
- 2 Corinthians 10:3-5
- Hebrews 4:12

TOOL'S, NOT
TOYS

Some of the pictures of Father Christmas in our world make him
look only funny and jolly. But now that the children actually
stood looking at him they didn't find it quite like that.
He was so big, and so glad, and so real, that they all became
quite still. They felt very glad, but also solemn.

"I've come at last," said he. "She has kept me out
for a long time, but I have got in at last. Aslan is on the move. . . ."

"Peter, Adam's Son," said Father Christmas.

"Here, sir," said Peter.

"These are your presents," was the answer, "and they are tools not toys.
The time to use them is perhaps near at hand. Bear them well."

Peter's gift is a sword and a shield. Susan receives a bow and a quiver of arrows and a horn to summon help in time of distress. Lucy is given a dagger she can use to defend herself and a cordial that will bring healing to those who are sick or wounded. These Christmas gifts are not toys, not playthings. They are tools and weapons. The children are being equipped for war. Soon they will take part in a great battle between good and evil, a battle for Narnia's deliverance. The gifts the children have been given will help them to fulfill their calling and to face the challenges that lie ahead.

The Bible tells us that there truly is a battle between good and evil raging constantly all around us, even when we're not aware of it. This spiritual warfare is all too real. And as C. S. Lewis once explained, "There is no neutral ground in the universe. Every square inch, every split second, is claimed by God and counterclaimed by Satan."

Ephesians 6:11-12 urges us: "Put on the full armor of God so that you can take your stand against the devil's schemes. For our struggle is not against flesh and blood, but against the rulers, against the authorities, against the powers of this dark world and against the spiritual forces of evil in the heavenly realms." The armor of God includes, among other things, the helmet of salvation, the sword of the Spirit, and the shield of faith (Ephesians 6:14-17).

The Scripture tells us that in addition to the "armor" that equips us for spiritual warfare, every believer is also given spiritual gifts. These gifts are supernatural talents, skills, and abilities that enable us to build up the Body of Christ, fulfill our calling, and face all the challenges we encounter in our adventure of faith.

Jesus sends these spiritual gifts through the Holy Spirit, and the Spirit gives them "to each man [and woman], just as he determines" (1 Corinthians 12:11). Each believer has his or her own special gift and calling. Some are given gifts of leadership and administration; others are given gifts of faith, wisdom, or discernment. Some have "gifts of healing" and the ability to help others.

Just as Father Christmas instructed the children about their gifts, the gifts we've been given are "tools not toys." It's our responsibility to discover what our gifts are, respect them, strengthen and develop them, and put them to use on the battlefield.

Sin doesn't bring us the rewards it promises.

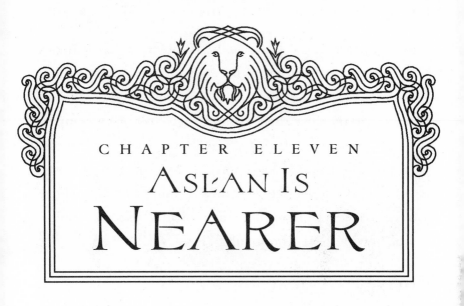

CHAPTER ELEVEN

ASLAN IS
NEARER

See! The winter is past; the rains are over and gone.

Flowers appear on the earth; the season of singing has come,

the cooing of doves is heard in our land.

SONG OF SONGS 2:11-12

BIBLICAL PARALLELS AND PRINCIPLES

~ Edmund's eyes are opened, and he begins to see the White Witch for who she really is. Psalm 5:9 says of the wicked, "Not a word from their mouth can be trusted; their heart is filled with destruction. Their throat is an open grave; with their tongue they speak deceit."

~ The Witch does not have a drop of kindness or compassion in her entire being. She even mistreats the reindeer that pull her sleigh. Proverbs 12:10 observes, "A righteous man cares for the needs of his animal, but the kindest acts of the wicked are cruel."

~ For the first time Edmund feels pity—or compassion—for someone besides himself. The Scriptures tell us, "Each of you should look not only to your own interests, but also to the interests of others" (Philippians 2:4). "Love one another" (1 John 4:7). "Rejoice with those who rejoice; mourn with those who mourn" (Romans 12:15).

DO YOU KNOW?

It becomes clear that the enchantment is broken—the Witch's power is crumbling. The Dwarf exclaims, "This is Aslan's doing!" The Bible says that Someone came to our world to destroy the works of the devil. Do you know who? (Hint: Read 1 John 3:8.)

SCRIPTURES ON CELEBRATING GOD'S DELIVERANCE

- Psalm 98
- Joel 2:21-27
- Revelation 15:3-4

CHAPTER TWELVE

PETER'S FIRST
BATTLE

So be strong, show yourself a man.

1 KINGS 2:2

BIBLICAL PARALLELS AND PRINCIPLES

~ Compare the description of the creatures gathered around Aslan at the pavilion to these verses: "In that day the Root of Jesse will stand as a banner for the peoples; the nations will rally to him, and his place of rest will be glorious" (Isaiah 11:10). "Your procession has come into view, O God. . . . In front are the singers, after them the musicians; with them are the maidens playing the tambourines" (Psalm 68:24-25). "Let every creature praise his holy name for ever and ever" (Psalm 145:21). Some readers may also be reminded of the

*We must learn to be strong
and courageous, ready for battle.*

scenes in Isaiah, Ezekiel, Daniel, and Revelation, which describe the fantastic beings who surround God's heavenly throne. These include seraphim and cherubim and other supernatural creatures that appear like leopards, lions, bears, eagles, oxen, and men.(For example, see Isaiah 6:1-3; Ezekiel 1:4-14; Revelation 4:6-8.)

~ Aslan is both "good and terrible at the same time." Years ago the word *terrible* was used to mean "frightening" or "awe-inspiring." The Scriptures tell us that people who had an encounter with the Living God nearly always responded in fear and reverence.(For one example, see Hebrews 12:21.) In the King James Version, Deuteronomy 7:21 explains, "The LORD thy God is among you, a mighty God and terrible." And Psalm 99:3 (KJV) says, "Let them praise thy great and terrible name; for it is holy." (Modern Bible translations replace the word "terrible" with "awesome.")

~ Aslan calls his servants to take the weary, worn-out girls and "minister" to them. After Jesus had endured temptation in the wilderness, God's servants—angels—were called to minister to Him (Matthew 4:11, ESV).

~ Peter faces his first test. Aslan ensures that Peter has the opportunity to begin developing the courage, maturity, and leadership ability that he will need as High King. God does the same for each one of us, preparing us for service in His kingdom. Psalm 18:34-38 says in part, "He trains my hands for battle; my arms can bend a bow of bronze. . . .

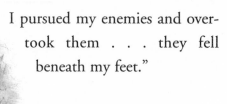

I pursued my enemies and overtook them . . . they fell beneath my feet."

Do You Know?

Some literary scholars have compared the Stone Table to ancient altars at sites of pagan worship, such as Stonehenge. But in a letter to a girl named Patricia, C. S. Lewis wrote that it was meant to remind readers of the stone table (or tablet) that God gave to Moses. Do you remember what that table (tablet) had written on it? (Hint: Read Exodus 24:12; Deuteronomy 10:4 and/or Exodus 20:1-17.)

SCRIPTURES ON COURAGE IN BATTLE

- Joshua 1:9
- Psalm 27:1-3
- Isaiah 12:2

WINNING OUR SPURS

"It is your sister's horn," said Aslan to Peter in a low voice;
so low as to be almost a purr,
if it is not disrespectful to think of a Lion purring.

For a moment Peter did not understand. Then, when he saw
all the other creatures start forward and heard Aslan say
with a wave of his paw, "Back! Let the Prince win his spurs,"
he did understand, and set off running as hard as he
could to the pavilion. And there he saw a dreadful sight. . . .

Peter did not feel very brave; indeed, he felt he was going to be sick.
But that made no difference to what he had to do. He rushed
straight up to the monster and aimed a slash of his sword at its side.

Aslan could have rescued Susan himself. The other creatures who had gathered around the pavilion could have fought off the wolf. But Aslan gave Peter the responsibility of coming to his sister's defense. This was Peter's chance to "win his spurs"to earn his knighthood. Aslan wanted to make sure that Peter had the opportunity to begin developing the courage, maturity, and leadership skills that he would need as Narnia's High King. Peter had been given a sword, and it was time for him to learn how to use it.

The Bible tells us it was a lot like that for David. As a shepherd boy, he learned to defend his flock first from a lion and then a bear (1 Samuel 17). He discovered that God was with him and that God would help him defeat his enemies. "It is God who arms me with strength. . . . He trains my hands for battle; my arms can bend a bow of bronze" (Psalm 18:32-34).

The confidence and courage that came from these experiences later enabled David to rise up against Goliath and knock the blaspheming giant flat on his face. Then the victory over Goliath gave David the courage to take on the entire Philistine army. One battle led to another. One victory led to another. And all along the way, God was working in the process: preparing David—equipping him—to become Israel's mightiest warrior and greatest king.

God does the same for each one of us. He is constantly working in every believer's life. He's teaching us, training us, preparing us to do the work of His kingdom. Often the most

effective method is to put obstacles in our path, give us bat-
tles to fight, challenges or trials we must learn to overcome.
And as—by God's grace—we conquer them, we grow
stronger and wiser and more confident in our calling. We
discover the reality of His presence and power in our lives.
That's why James could exclaim, "Consider it pure joy, my
brothers, whenever you face trials of many kinds, because
you know that the testing of your faith develops perseverance. Perseverance must finish its work so that you may be
mature and complete, not lacking anything" (James 1:2-4).

Instead of being discouraged when difficulties arise, we
must learn to see them for what they are: opportunities for
us to "win our spurs." By God's grace and in His strength,
we can learn to triumph over our troubles and turn them
one by one into spiritual victories.

Even when things seem hopeless,
God can make a way.

CHAPTER THIRTEEN

DEEP MAGIC FROM THE DAWN OF TIME

*Against you, you only, have I sinned and done
what is evil in your sight, so that you are proved right
when you speak and justified when you judge.*

PSALM 51:4

BIBLICAL PARALLELS AND PRINCIPLES

~ Aslan says that there is no need to speak of Edmund's earlier behavior. He has been forgiven. Isaiah 43:18 tells us, "Forget the former things; do not dwell on the past." In verse 25 God explains, "I, even I, I am he who blots out your transgressions . . . and remembers your sins no more."

~During the encounter with the White Witch, Edmund keeps his eyes on Aslan. Psalm 105:4 says, "Look to the LORD and his strength; seek his face always." Psalm 34:5 explains, "Those who look to him are radiant; their faces are never covered with shame."

~ As a traitor, Edmund stands condemned. "All who sin under the law will be judged by the law" (Romans 2:12). "The wages of sin is death" (Romans 6:23). Hebrews 9:22 explains, "Without the shedding of blood there is no forgiveness of sins" (ESV). "It is the blood that makes atonement" (Leviticus 17:11).

~ Notice Aslan's response to Susan's suggestion that he work against the Emperor's Magic. In Matthew 5:17-18 Jesus said, "Do not think that I have come to abolish the Law or the Prophets; I have not come to abolish them but to fulfill them. I tell you the truth, until heaven and earth disappear, not the smallest letter, not the least stroke of a pen, will by any means disappear from the Law until everything is accomplished."

~ The punishment for Edmund's sin cannot be ignored, forgotten, or suspended somehow. The penalty must be paid—and Aslan takes that responsibility upon himself. Isaiah 53:4 says of Jesus, "Surely he took up our infirmities and carried our sorrows." First Peter 2:24 says, "He himself bore our sins."

~ As "the Emperor's hangman," the Witch cruelly delights in carrying out judgment against those who have sinned. Whether she recognizes it or not, it is still the Emperor's judgment she carries out—ultimately, it is his purpose she is serving. The Scripture tells us that Satan's authority comes from God, and that his power is limited by God. (See Isaiah 54:16-17; Job 1—2; Luke 22:31-32; 1 John 4:4.) Though the devil would love nothing more than to destroy God and His people, he cannot. He is merely a tool that ultimately serves God's purposes.

THINK ABOUT IT!

Though the White Witch calls herself "Queen," she has no right to the title. Soon, Aslan says, all names will be restored to "their proper owners." John 14:30 refers to Satan as "the prince of this world." The devil represents himself as its ruler (Luke 4:5-6). But who is really the Prince? (Hint: Read Acts 5:30-31 and Isaiah 9:6-7.)

SCRIPTURES ON THE LAW

- Psalm 19:7-10
- Isaiah 42:21
- Matthew 22:35-40

Jesus took the punishment in our place.

CHAPTER FOURTEEN

THE TRIUMPH
OF THE WITCH

Greater love has no one than this,
that he lay down his life for his friends.

JOHN 15:13

BIBLICAL PARALLELS AND PRINCIPLES

~ Compare Aslan's sorrow and desire for companionship to Matthew 26:36-38. Jesus took three of His closest disciples with Him as He went to Gethsemane to pray. "He began to be sorrowful and troubled. Then he said to them, 'My soul is overwhelmed with sorrow to the point of death. Stay here and keep watch with me.'"

~ Aslan offers no resistance when attacked by the evil creatures. He says nothing in answer to their taunts.

Speaking prophetically of Jesus, Isaiah 53:7 says, "He was oppressed and afflicted, yet he did not open his mouth; he was led like a lamb to the slaughter, and as a sheep before her shearers is silent, so he did not open his mouth." (See also Matthew 26:62-63a; 27:13-14; Luke 23:8-9.)

~ The creatures cruelly abuse Aslan—just as wicked men abused Jesus. "They spit in his face and struck him with their fists. Others slapped him and said, 'Prophesy to us, Christ. Who hit you?'" (Matthew 26:67). They plucked out His beard (Isaiah 50:6-7). The Roman soldiers stripped Him and flogged Him. They made Him wear a scarlet robe and "wove a crown of thorns and set it on his head" (Matthew 27:29). Then they knelt in front of Him, saying "Hail, King of the Jews!" They spit on Him; they "struck him on the head again and again" (Matthew 27:29-30). Then they led Him away to be crucified.

~ It seems that evil has triumphed and all hope is lost—certainly Jesus' disciples thought so when He died on the cross. But Jesus, predicting His crucifixion, saw it differently. "The hour has come for the Son of Man to be glorified. . . . Now my heart is troubled, and what shall I say? 'Father, save me from this hour'? No, it was for this very reason I came" (John 12:23, 27-28).

SOUND FAMILIAR?

Susan and Lucy were the only ones to witness Aslan's suffering and sacrifice. When Jesus was crucified, most of His disciples were in hiding—afraid that they might be next. But a faithful group of women kept watch at the foot of the cross. Do you remember who? (Hint: Read Matthew 27:55-56; Mark 15:40; John 19:25.)

SCRIPTURES ON CHRIST'S SUFFERING AND SACRIFICE

- Isaiah 53
- 1 John 4:10
- 1 Peter 2:21-25

GREATER L'OVE
HAS NO ONE
THAN THIS

"Have you forgotten the Deep Magic?" asked the Witch.

"Let us say I have forgotten it," answered Aslan gravely.
"Tell us of this Deep Magic."

"Tell you?" said the Witch, her voice growing suddenly shriller.
"Tell you what is written on the very Table of Stone which
stands beside us? Tell you what is written in letters as deep as a spear
is long on the fire-stones on the Secret Hill? Tell you what is
engraved on the scepter of the Emperor-beyond-the-Sea? You at least
know the Magic which the Emperor put into Narnia at the very
beginning. You know that every traitor belongs to me as my lawful
prey and that for every treachery I have a right to a kill."

"Please—Aslan," said Lucy,
"can anything be done to save Edmund?"

"All shall be done," said Aslan.
"But it may be harder than you think."

"Fall back, all of you," said Aslan. "and I will talk to the Witch
alone." They all obeyed. It was a terrible time this—waiting
and wondering while the Lion and the Witch talked
earnestly together in low voices. . . .

At last they heard Aslan's voice.
"You can all come back," he said. "I have settled the matter.
She has renounced the claim on your brother's blood."

The Deep Magic—the law on which Narnia was founded—cannot be ignored or escaped or abolished. It must be fulfilled, or else "all Narnia will be overturned and perish in fire and water." A treachery has been committed, and someone must pay the price. Edmund is the one who deserves to die. He is, after all, the one who betrayed his own brother and sisters. But Aslan comes to his rescue. To save Edmund's life, Aslan will give up his own. It is the ultimate sacrifice.

Jesus said, "Greater love has no one than this, that he lay down his life for his friends" (John 15:13). The ultimate sacrifice is one that Jesus willingly made for us. "I lay down my life," He told His disciples in the days before His cruci-fixion. "No one takes it from me, but I lay it down of my own accord" (John 10:17-18).

Why would anyone do such a thing? Why would any-one purposely, willingly endure such excruciating torture, such an agonizing death?

"Very rarely will anyone die for a righteous man, though for a good man someone might possibly dare to die. But God demonstrates his own love for us in this: While we were still sinners, Christ died for us" (Romans 5:7-8).

It was all about love. Love for you. Love for me. Love for all mankind.

We did nothing to deserve this love. We weren't inno-cent victims. We were sinners, traitors—guilty as charged. The Scripture says, "All who sin under the law will be judged by the law" (Romans 2:12). The just penalty for our sin was death.

But "God made him who had no sin to be sin for us" (2 Corinthians 5:21).

Jesus willingly—lovingly—took the punishment in our place.

"Surely he took up our infirmities and carried our sor-rows . . . he was pierced for our transgressions, he was crushed for our iniquities; the punishment that brought us peace was upon him, and by his wounds we are healed" (Isaiah 53:4-5).

CHAPTER FIFTEEN

DEEPER MAGIC FROM BEFORE THE DAWN OF TIME

There was a violent earthquake, for an angel
of the Lord came down from heaven and, going to the tomb,
rolled back the stone and sat on it.

MATTHEW 28:2

BIBLICAL PARALLELS AND PRINCIPLES

~ The girls tenderly care for Aslan's bruised and broken body. Mice nibble away at the ropes that bind him. Similarly, Jesus' friends showed tender concern for His earthly body. Joseph of Arimathea took His body down from the cross (John 19:38-42). The women went to the tomb at sunrise to anoint His body with spices (Mark 16:1-2).

Death is not the end of the story.

~ Hearing a noise behind them, Susan and Lucy think that someone has disturbed Aslan's body. The Bible tells us that when Mary Magdalene found His tomb empty, she thought someone must have removed Jesus' body. "They have taken my Lord away," she wept. Then a voice behind her spoke. She turned around, and there stood Jesus Himself (John 20:10-16).

~ Susan fears that they are seeing a ghost. Jesus' disciples felt the same way when He first appeared to them after His resurrection (Luke 24:37-39). Jesus reassured them that it really was Him—in a glorified body that still bore the marks of His crucifixion. "Jesus said, 'Peace be with you!' . . . And with that he breathed on them" (John 20:21-22).

~ Aslan talks about the Deep Magic and the Emperor's Deeper Magic. The apostle Paul explained the deeper meaning behind Jesus' death on the cross by saying, "We do, however, speak a message of wisdom among the mature, but not the wisdom of this age or of the rulers of this age, who are coming to nothing. No, we speak of God's secret wisdom, a wisdom that has been hidden and that God destined for our glory before time began. None of the rulers of this age understood it, for if they had, they would not have crucified the Lord of glory" (1 Corinthians 2:6-8).

~ The Deeper Magic stated that "when a willing victim who had committed no treachery was killed in a traitor's stead, the Table would crack and Death itself would start working backward." Romans 5:7-8 observes, "Very rarely will anyone die for a righteous man, though for a good man someone might possibly dare to die. But God demonstrates his love for us in this: While we were still sinners, Christ died for us." He Himself had committed no sin; instead, He bore our sins (1 Peter 2:22-24). Galatians 3:13 says, "Christ redeemed us from the curse of the law." According to Isaiah 53:5, He was wounded for our transgressions—He took the punishment for our sin, "and by his wounds we are healed." First Corinthians 15:54 declares, "Death has been swallowed up in victory."

~ As Aslan said, "Death itself would start working backward." After his resurrection Aslan heads straight for the Witch's castle, where he will set free those she has held captive and turned to stone. The Bible tells us that as Jesus completed His atoning work on the cross, "The tombs broke open and the bodies of many holy people who had died were raised to life" (Matthew 27:52). Also, during the time between His death and resurrection, Jesus descended into Hades and preached to the righteous who were imprisoned there (awaiting His atonement). He set the captives free and led them into Heaven (1 Peter 3:19; Ephesians 4:8-10)

SOUND FAMILIAR?

When Aslan willingly laid down his life for Edmund, the Stone Table broke in two. When Jesus willingly laid down

His life for us, the spiritual barrier between God and man was destroyed—and a physical symbol of that barrier was torn in two. Do you remember what that symbol was? (Hint: Read Matthew 27:51.)

SCRIPTURES ON THE ATONING WORK OF CHRIST

- John 3:16-17
- Romans 3:23-26
- Hebrews 9:14

THE LION ROARS

"Oh, you're real, you're real! Oh, Aslan!" cried Lucy,
and both girls flung themselves upon him and covered him with kisses.

"But what does it all mean?"
asked Susan when they were somewhat calmer.

"It means," said Aslan, "that though the Witch knew the Deep Magic,
there is a magic deeper still which she did not know.
Her knowledge goes back only to the dawn of time. But if she could
have looked a little further back, into the stillness and the
darkness before Time dawned, she would have read there a different
incantation. She would have known that when a willing victim
who had committed no treachery was killed in a traitor's stead, the
Table would crack and Death itself would start working backward."

At first it seemed as though the Witch had triumphed. With her own two hands, she had tortured and killed Aslan at the Stone Table. Susan and Lucy witnessed the whole thing. They watched him die. And yet he lives!

The women who had watched Jesus die could not believe that His body was not to be found in the tomb. But the angel told them, "He is not here; he has risen, just as he said" (Matthew 28:6).

Aslan explains to Susan and Lucy that there is a Deeper Magic—a greater law—at work. One that the Witch did not know.

Explaining the meaning behind Jesus' death on the cross, the apostle Paul said, "We do, however, speak a message of wisdom among the mature, but not the wisdom of this age or of the rulers of this age, who are coming to nothing. No, we speak of God's secret wisdom, a wisdom that has been hidden and that God destined for our glory before time began. None of the rulers of this age understood it, for if they had, they would not have crucified the Lord of glory" (1 Corinthians 2:6-8).

They had no idea that by crucifying Jesus, they were actually making it possible for Him to accomplish what He had come to earth to do. "Christ redeemed us from the curse of the law" (Galatians 3:13). With His sacrifice, Jesus set us free from the power of sin and death. He made it possible for us to be reconciled to God, restored to a right relationship with Him, and given the gift of eternal life.

But because Jesus Himself was without sin—because He had done nothing to deserve to die—death had no legal hold on Him. It could not keep Him in the grave. He rose from the dead in power and glory. "Death has been swallowed up in victory" (1 Corinthians 15:54). "[God] has rescued us from the dominion of darkness and brought us into the kingdom of the Son he loves, in whom we have redemption, the forgiveness of sins" (Colossians 1:13-14).

Jesus snatched victory from the jaws of defeat, turning a day of tragedy into an eternal triumph. The Lion of Judah roared!

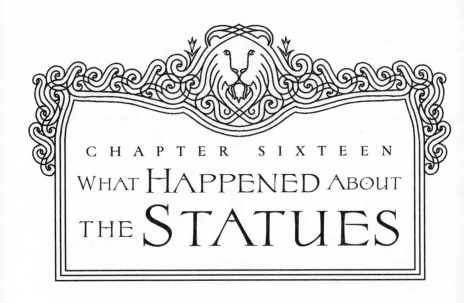

CHAPTER SIXTEEN
WHAT HAPPENED ABOUT THE STATUES

The lion has roared.

AMOS 3:8

BIBLICAL PARALLELS AND PRINCIPLES

~ Death starts working backward—Aslan's breath brings the statues to life. When the first human being was created, "The LORD God . . . breathed into his nostrils the breath of life" (Genesis 2:7). In Ezekiel 37:5 God speaks to the slain in the Valley of Bones: "I will make breath enter you, and you will come to life." John 20:22 tells us that after His resurrection, Jesus breathed on His disciples. (For more on the new life that resulted from the Resurrection, see Matthew 27:52 and the notes on Chapter Fifteen of this book.)

Evil cannot triumph.
Victory belongs to God.

~ Alive again, Aslan begins to go about "setting wrongs to right." When He began His earthly ministry, Jesus quoted Isaiah 61:1-2 (a prophecy concerning Himself and His calling): "The Spirit of the Sovereign LORD is on me, because the LORD has anointed me to preach good news to the poor. He has sent me to bind up the brokenhearted, to proclaim freedom for the captives and release from darkness for the prisoners, to proclaim the year of the LORD's favor and the day of vengeance of our God."

~ With a mighty roar, Aslan leads the Narnian creatures on to war against the Witch. Isaiah 31:4 says, "As a lion growls, a great lion over his prey . . . so the LORD Almighty will come down to do battle." "Like a warrior he will stir up his zeal; with a shout he will raise the battle cry and will triumph over his enemies" (Isaiah 42:13).

~ The Lion has triumphed (Revelation 5:5). The White Witch is defeated. "You said, 'I will continue forever—the eternal queen!' But you did not consider these things or reflect on what might happen" (Isaiah 47:7). "Rejoice over her, O heaven! Rejoice, saints and apostles and prophets! God has judged her for the way she treated you" (Revelation 18:20).

DO YOU KNOW?

The Narnian creatures must fight a vast, supernaturally evil army. The Bible tells us that as believers, we are all engaged in an ongoing battle. Who or what is the enemy? (Hint: Read Ephesians 6:11-12.)

SCRIPTURES ON JOY

- Psalm 16:11
- Psalm 66:1-4
- Psalm 126:1-3

CHAPTER SEVENTEEN

THE HUNTING OF THE WHITE STAG

Blessed is the man who perseveres under trial,
because when he has stood the test, he will receive the crown of life
that God has promised to those who love him.

JAMES 1:12

BIBLICAL PARALLELS AND PRINCIPLES

~ Unlike Judas in the Bible, Edmund has repented of his sin. He is forgiven and restored to a right relationship with Aslan and his own brother and sisters. In fact, as Lucy observes, he has become a changed person. In Ezekiel 36:26 God says, "I will give you a new heart and put a new spirit in you; I will remove from you your heart of stone and give you a heart of flesh."

We can't even begin to imagine
the joys God has in store for us.

~ Lucy's trust in and obedience to Aslan is tested when he asks her to leave Edmund's side and care for others. Sometimes God asks us to do things we don't want to do. In John 14:15 Jesus said, "If you love me, you will obey what I command." He promises that those who trust in Him will never be put to shame (Romans 10:11).

~ On a grassy hillside, Aslan miraculously provides food for the entire company. The Bible tells us that Jesus miraculously fed five thousand people on a grassy hillside with five loaves of bread and two small fish. (See Matthew 14:15-21, Mark 6:35-44, Luke 9:12-17, or John 6:1-14.)

~ Aslan comes and goes—suddenly and mysteriously— just as Jesus did after His resurrection. (For various instances, see Matthew 28:9; Mark 16:9-14; Luke 24:15, 36; John 20:14, 19, 26; 21:1, 4) Mr. Beaver explains that Aslan has "other countries to attend to." Jesus compared Himself to a shepherd and told His disciples, "I have other sheep that are not of this sheep pen. I must bring them also. They too will listen to my voice, and there shall be one flock and one shepherd" (John 10:16).

DO YOU KNOW?

Though Edmund was "a sneak and a traitor," Aslan suffered and died to save him from the power of the White Witch. Lucy asks Susan, "Does he know what Aslan did for him?"

Do you know what Jesus did for you? (Hint: Read Romans 5:8; 1 John 2:2; and Isaiah 53:4-5.)

SCRIPTURES ON THE GLORY THAT AWAITS US

- 1 Peter 2:9
- 2 Corinthians 3:18
- Revelation 22:1-5

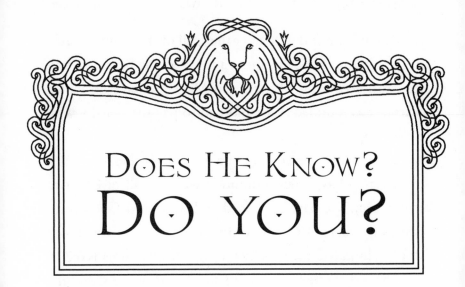

DOES HE KNOW?
DO YOU?

*"Does he know," whispered Lucy to Susan, "what Aslan did for him?
Does he know what the arrangement with the Witch really was?"*

"Hush! No, of course not," said Susan.

"Oughtn't he to be told?" said Lucy.

*"Oh, surely not," said Susan. "It would be too awful for him.
Think how you'd feel if you were he."*

"All the same I think he ought to know," said Lucy.

Edmund's salvation came at a great price.
So did yours and mine.

When Edmund fell under the spell of the White Witch, he gave in to pride, selfishness, and greed. He became a traitor. And according to the Deep Magic, or law, on which Narnia was founded, Edmund had to pay the penalty with his life.

The Bible tells us that at one time or another, every one of us has behaved like Edmund. We have all given in to temptation. We have all sinned and disobeyed God's commands (Romans 3:23). According to the law on which our world is founded, the penalty for sin is death (Romans 6:23).

The only hope for Edmund and Narnia was Aslan—the Lord of the Wood, the King of Beasts, Son of the Emperor-Beyond-the-Sea. Only Aslan could save Edmund and Narnia from the power of the White Witch.

The only hope for us is Jesus—the "Lion of Judah"—the King of kings, Lord of lords, Son of God. He is the only One who can save us from our sin. That's why He came to earth. "The reason the Son of God appeared was to destroy the devil's work" (1 John 3:8).

Aslan laid down his own life for Edmund, taking Edmund's punishment and dying in his place. The Bible says, "This is how we know what love is: Jesus Christ laid down his life for us" (1 John 3:16a).

By suffering a horrible, agonizing death on the Stone Table, Aslan set Narnia and Edmund free. For there was an even "Deeper Magic"—a greater law—at work: "When a willing victim who had committed no treachery was killed in a traitor's stead, the Table would crack and Death itself would start working backward." With Aslan's sacrifice, the curse was broken.

The Bible tells us that by suffering a horrible, agonizing death on the cross, Jesus set creation and all humankind free. With His sacrifice, the power of sin and death was broken. "'Where, O death, is your victory? Where, O death, is your sting?' The sting of death is sin, and the power of sin is the law. But thanks be to God! He gives us the victory through our Lord Jesus Christ" (1 Corinthians 15:55-57).

Just as Aslan rose from the dead in Narnia, Jesus Christ rose from the dead in our world. One day we will live forever with Him in Heaven—a place so perfect, so wonderful, so fabulous that words fail to describe it (1 Corinthians 2:9)!

Now you know what Jesus has done for you.

What will you do for Him? Will you thank Him for His sacrifice? Will you give Him your love and your life in return? You might pray something like this:

Dear Jesus, I know that I'm a sinner. Please forgive me for all the wrong things I've ever said or done. Thank You for dying on the cross for my sins. Thank You for breaking the curse and setting me free. Come live in my heart. Help me to live my life in a way that pleases You. Amen.

CONTINUING THE ADVENTURE

There are many ways you can continue your own adventures in Narnia—activities, crafts, and projects that will help you celebrate your favorite moments in the story. In the following pages you will find a few ideas to get you started.

TEA WITH MR. TUMNUS

When Mr. Tumnus meets Lucy in the forest, he invites her to tea. In England, "tea" is more than a hot drink. The word often refers to a light meal served at 3 or 4 o'clock in the afternoon—in between an early lunch and a late dinner. Just for fun, invite your family and friends or classmates to join you for tea. If you want to, you can serve soft-boiled eggs and sardines on toast, as Mr. Tumnus did. Here are some other traditional and tasty treats your guests will enjoy:

Small sandwiches—made on thin bread, with the crusts removed—cut into triangles or squares

A variety of cookies, cakes, scones, and fruit tarts

HOW TO MAKE A POT OF TEA

You will need one tea bag for each cup of water—usually 3-4 tea bags per teapot. You can use an ordinary black tea, such as orange pekoe, or a flavored herb tea.

Directions:

1. Bring cold water to a full boil, either in a kettle or a saucepan on the stove.

2. Pour the boiling water over the tea bags in a teapot. (You may want to ask an adult to help you.)

3. Let the tea brew for 4-5 minutes.

4. Serve with lemon or milk and sugar.

HOW TO MAKE ENGLISH SCONES

This delicious pastry is sort of a cross between a cookie and a muffin. The following recipe makes 10-12 scones.

Ingredients:

2 cups all-purpose flour

2/3 cup granulated sugar

4 oz. butter or margarine

1/4 cup shortening

1 whole egg
1/2 cup raisins

For Step Four:

1 lightly beaten egg
1 tbsp sugar

Directions:

1. Mix all ingredients together by hand. If they aren't blending well, add a splash of milk.
2. Pat out dough to 1/2-inch thickness; cut into circles with a cookie cutter or jar lid.
3. Bake for 8-10 minutes at 400° on an ungreased cookie sheet.
4. Flip scones over, brush tops with beaten egg, and sprinkle with sugar; bake another 8-10 minutes until lightly brown.
5. Allow the scones to cool completely; serve plain or topped with a dollop of butter.

Another way to celebrate: Arrange to host a party at an authentic British tearoom. Go online or look in the phone book to find a tearoom near you. Be sure to call ahead for information and reservations. Some tearooms invite you to come in costume or formal dress, while others are more casual. At certain times of year there may be special group rates, educational events, or seasonal celebrations.

EDMUND'S TURKISH DELIGHT

When the Witch offered Edmund anything he wanted to eat, he chose Turkish Delight—a gooey kind of sugarcoated, fruit-flavored candy that is very popular in England and other European countries. If you'd like to try it, ask an adult to help you with this recipe. Unlike the enchanted kind, this candy is only delicious, not dangerous!

Ingredients:

- 2 cups granulated sugar
- 1 1/4 cups water
- 1 lemon peel (cut into strips; the juice squeezed and strained)
- 1 orange peel (cut into strips; the juice squeezed and strained)
- 4 tbsp unflavored powdered gelatin
- 2 tbsp powdered sugar
- 1 tbsp cornstarch

Directions:

1. Dissolve the sugar in the water in a saucepan on medium heat.
2. Add the strips of lemon and orange peel and the juices. Bring to a boil and simmer for fifteen minutes.
3. Soak the gelatin in the mixture for 5-10 minutes; strain into a shallow pan or platter. Let it set for 24 hours.
4. Cut the candy into one-inch squares.

5. Sift the cornstarch and powdered sugar together in a shallow dish; roll the pieces of candy into the mixture and serve. (If you want to save some for later, store the leftover pieces in layers separated by wax paper, covered with an extra sprinkling of the cornstarch and powdered sugar mixture.)

If you don't have time to cook, stop by a grocery store that has a wide selection of ethnic or exotic foods—or check the phone book for a British goods/groceries import store. You'll find beautifully wrapped boxes of prepackaged Turkish Delight in the candy aisle. You may also be able to order it online.

MAKE THE STORY YOUR OWN

There are many ways to make this wonderful tale a part of your life.

Draw a map of Narnia. Trace the journeys of the main characters, or mark the locations where important things took place. Your map can be as small as a sheet of notebook paper or as large as a poster you hang on the wall.

Create your own collection of poems inspired by characters or events in the book. Put them together in a booklet or journal that you decorate yourself.

Decorate your room with your own handmade snowflakes. Hang them from the ceiling with pushpins and yarn or curling ribbon.

Write a letter to a friend, as if you are one of the main characters, such as Peter or Lucy or Mr. Tumnus. Tell them the story as if it happened to you.

Choose a scene from the book, and ask a few friends or classmates to act it out with you. Use props and costumes if you want to—or just use your imagination. Practice several times on your own, and then perform the scene for others.

Make a model of an object such as the wardrobe, the Witch's house, the Beavers' Dam, or the castle of Cair Paravel. Or create a diorama, a display with miniature figures and objects representing an important scene from the story.

Design a series of bookmarks, each one featuring a specific person, place, or thing from the book. On the front, draw a picture of the subject. On the back, write a description, explaining its importance to the story. Give the bookmarks as gifts to your friends and family—or keep them for yourself!

READ THE OTHER BOOKS IN THE SERIES

Other books in *The Chronicles of Narnia* by C. S. Lewis include:

Book One: *The Magician's Nephew*
Book Three: *The Horse and His Boy*
Book Four: *Prince Caspian*
Book Five: *The Voyage of the Dawn Treader*

Book Six: *The Silver Chair*
Book Seven: *The Last Battle*

The Lion, the Witch and the Wardrobe was the first book C. S. Lewis wrote about Narnia. Later he wrote six more, including a prequel explaining how the world of Narnia came to be. At Lewis's suggestion, publishers renumbered the series to reflect the chronological order of the stories rather than the publication date. Read on to learn why Professor Kirke has no trouble believing the children's story about the wardrobe and what other adventures await Peter, Susan, Edmund, and Lucy in Narnia.

Book One: *The Magician's Nephew:* Mad scientist or magician Andrew Ketterly gives his nephew, Digory Kirke, and neighbor-girl, Polly, two magic rings that will transport them into world after world beyond our own. Digory hopes he'll find a cure that will save his dying mother. Instead he meets a Great Lion who sends him on an important quest. Will Digory obey Aslan's instructions, even when he doesn't understand—or will he listen to the secrets of a sorceress who promises to fulfill his wildest dreams?

Book Three: *The Horse and His Boy:* Peter rules as High King over Narnia, and his brother and sisters sit as King and Queens under him on the four thrones of Cair Paravel. Meanwhile, in Calormen to the south an orphaned peasant boy, a nobleman's daughter, and two talking horses plan a daring escape from a land of slavery. As their journey begins, the runaways uncover a treacherous plot that could spell disaster for Narnia and all of its creatures. Will they manage to warn the Kings and Queens in time?

Book Four: *Prince Caspian:* On their way back to school after the holidays, the four Pevensie children suddenly find themselves back in Narnia—where it has been a thousand years since they first reigned. Dark times have fallen on their former kingdom. Evil men rule the land, and the Talking Beasts have gone into hiding. Young Prince Caspian wants to set things right, but he needs the Pevensies' help to defeat the wicked uncle who has stolen his throne.

Book Five: *The Voyage of the Dawn Treader:* Edmund, Lucy, and their cousin Eustace join King Caspian on an epic adventure to find the friends and nobles his Uncle Miraz banished from the kingdom long ago. Along the way they'll meet slave traders, sea serpents, and stars who walk the earth. And Reepicheep the mouse will urge them all on to the end of the world, where he hopes to find Aslan's Country.

Book Six: *The Silver Chair:* King Caspian is broken-hearted. His only son has disappeared. Prince Rilian was last seen in the company of a beautiful enchantress. Wise old Narnians believe the prince has been kidnapped by one of those "northern witches" who are always plotting to over-throw their country. The Great Lion Aslan sends Eustace and his schoolmate Jill on a quest to find and rescue the captive prince before it's too late.

Book Seven: *The Last Battle:* Eustace and Jill learn that King Tirian needs help. Narnia is falling into the hands of its deadly enemies, the Calormenes. And the one behind its surrender appears to be Aslan himself! This cruel and vicious taskmaster is nothing like the Great Lion in the stories of old. Is it possible that he has changed so much? Or is this a deadly deception that will lead to Narnia's destruction? Is there any hope that Narnia can be saved?

Just as in *The Lion, the Witch and the Wardrobe,* there are "stories within the stories"—profound spiritual truths and powerful life lessons in each of these books. Keep your eyes open, and see if you can discover them for yourself.

A LIST OF MAIN CHARACTERS

Peter Pevensie: The oldest of the four children, he is a born leader. He shows strength and courage, in addition to a love for adventure. Whether it's in seeking the professor's counsel, apologizing to Lucy, or planning the rescue of Mr. Tumnus and Edmund, Peter is always quick to do the right thing.

Susan Pevensie: As the oldest sister, she feels practically grown up. In her parents' absence, she watches over her brothers and sister and tries to keep everyone in line. Overly cautious, even fearful, Susan would rather avoid the unknown dangers that an adventure in Narnia presents—but her sense of duty and responsibility help her rise to the challenge.

Edmund Pevensie: A greedy, selfish, mean-spirited boy, he enjoys provoking his brother and sisters. Falling under the spell of the White Witch, he betrays them all—setting the stage for the most dramatic events of the story. His salvation comes at a great price.

Lucy Pevensie: The youngest of the four children, she is the first to discover Narnia by climbing into the wardrobe. Always truthful and very tenderhearted, she suffers a great deal when her brothers and sister don't believe her story. But because of her compassion for others, she is quick to forgive them—and anxious to rescue Mr. Tumnus and all the creatures of Narnia oppressed by the White Witch.

Professor Kirke: The gruff, old professor hosts the Pevensie children at his country home, where they have come to escape the air raids in London. His willingness to believe or at least accept Lucy's fantastic story surprises Peter and Susan.

Mr. Tumnus: The good-hearted faun befriends Lucy upon her arrival in Narnia. He intends to turn her over to the White Witch, as he has been ordered to do, but can't bring himself to go through with the awful deed. Instead, he helps Lucy escape.

The White Witch: The evil sorceress claims to be "Queen of Narnia." Her spell makes it "always winter and never Christmas." She will do anything to keep the four children from fulfilling the prophecies that signal the end of her reign.

Mr. Beaver: A friend of Mr. Tumnus, he meets the children in the forest and brings them back to his dam. There he explains Narnia's history and the prophecies that are about to be fulfilled, before taking the children to meet Aslan at the Stone Table.

Mrs. Beaver: The kindly, capable wife of Mr. Beaver, she welcomes the children into her home and feeds them a good, hot meal. Ever practical, she makes very thorough preparations for their long journey to the Stone Table.

Maugrim (Fenris Ulf): The vicious gray wolf is the Chief of the Witch's Secret Police. He arrests Mr. Tumnus for allowing Lucy to escape and later attacks Susan at the pavilion before falling to Peter's sword.

Father Christmas: The White Witch has kept him out of Narnia for years. When her spell begins to break, he arrives with gifts for the Pevensie children that will help them defeat the Witch's army on the battlefield.

Aslan: The Great Lion, the King of the Beasts, Lord of Narnia and all its creatures, Son of the Emperor-Over-the-Sea. Only Aslan can save Narnia from the power of the White Witch. Aslan is the one "behind all the stories" in *The Chronicles of Narnia.*

MAP OF NARNIA

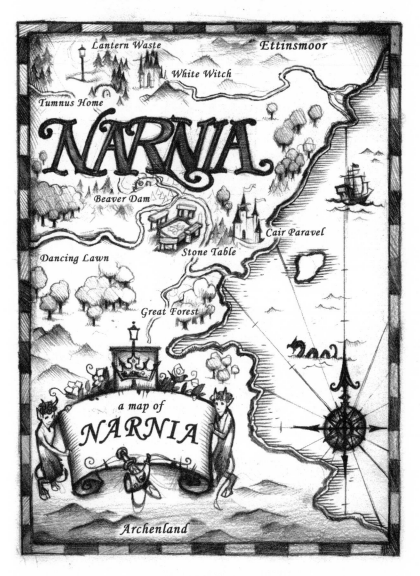

Lantern Waste

Ettinsmoor

White Witch

Tumnus Home

NARNIA

Beaver Dam

Cair Paravel

Stone Table

Dancing Lawn

Great Forest

a map of
NARNIA

Archenland

FIND OUT MORE

BOOKS ABOUT *THE CHRONICLES OF NARNIA*

Bruner, Kurt D. and Jim Ware. *Finding God in the Land of Narnia.* Wheaton, IL: Tyndale House Publishers, 2004.

Ditchfield, Christin. *A Family Guide to Narnia: Biblical Truths in C. S. Lewis's The Chronicles of Narnia.* Wheaton, IL: Crossway Books, 2003.

———. *A Christian Teacher's Guide to The Lion, the Witch and the Wardrobe.* Greensboro, NC: Carson-Dellosa Publishing Company, 2005.

Duriez, Colin. *A Field Guide to Narnia.* Downers Grove, IL: InterVarsity Press, 2004.

Ford, Paul F. *Companion to Narnia.* San Francisco: HarperCollins, 1994.

Sibley, Brian. *The Land of Narnia.* San Francisco: HarperCollins, 1998.

BOOKS ABOUT C. S. LEWIS

Bingham, Derick. *C. S. Lewis: The Story Teller.* Fearn, Scotland: Christian Focus Publications, 1999.

Cording, Ruth James. *C. S. Lewis: A Celebration of His Early Life.* Nashville: Broadman & Holman, 2000.

Dorsett, Lyle W. and Marjorie Lamp Mead. *C. S. Lewis: Letters to Children.* New York: Simon & Schuster, 1995.

Duriez, Colin. *Tolkien and C. S. Lewis: The Gift of Friendship.* Mahwah, NJ: Paulist Press, 2003.

Gresham, Douglas. *Lenten Lands: My Childhood with Joy Davidman and C. S. Lewis.* San Francisco: HarperCollins, 2003.

Peters, Thomas C. *Simply C. S. Lewis: A Beginner's Guide to the Life and Works of C. S. Lewis.* Wheaton, IL: Crossway Books, 1997.

Stone, Elaine Murray. *C. S. Lewis: Creator of Narnia.* Mahwah, NJ: Paulist Press, 2001.

WEBSITES FOR NARNIA FANS

The official site of *The Chronicles of Narnia:* www.narnia.com.

Explore the breathtaking fantasy world of C. S. Lewis on the Web: www.virtualnarnia.com.

The C. S. Lewis Foundation: www.cslewis.org.

The HarperCollins C. S. Lewis site: www.cslewisclassics.com.

OTHER MEDIA

The Chronicles Of Narnia: The Lion, the Witch and the Wardrobe. A movie by Walden/Disney, Christmas 2005. Information: www.walden.com.

The Lion, the Witch and the Wardrobe Bulletin Board Set by Carson-Dellosa. To order, call 800-321-0943 or visit www.carsondellosa.com.

The Lion, the Witch and the Wardrobe, Focus on the Family Radio Theatre, on cassette or compact disc. For more information, call 1-800-A-FAMILY.

PLACES TO VISIT

The Marion E. Wade Center at Wheaton College, Wheaton, IL 60187. This international study and research center houses the world's largest collection of C. S. Lewis's letters, manuscripts, audio and video tapes, dissertations, artwork, periodicals, photographs, and memorabilia. For information on tours, call 630-752-5908 or visit www.wheaton.edu/learners/wade/.

The Kilns at Oxford, England. Each year thousands of tourists visit C. S. Lewis's home in Oxfordshire, England. For photographs of the site and information on tours, visit www.cslewistours.co.uk.

Christin Ditchfield is the host of the internationally syndicated radio program *Take It To Heart!*™ She is an accomplished educator, a popular conference speaker, and the author of more than forty books—including Crossway's *A Family Guide to Narnia.* Christin's articles have been featured in numerous national and international magazines, such as *Focus on the Family, Today's Christian Woman, Sports Spectrum,* and *Power for Living.* She writes the "Everyday Theology" column for *Today's Christian* (formerly *Christian Reader*).

For more information, visit Christin's website at www.TakeItToHeartRadio.com.

Other Crossway books by Christin Ditchfield:

A Family Guide to Narnia

Take It To Heart

The Three Wise Women